Inspired by Nature

BUILDINGS
Inspired by Nature

by Mary Boone

PEBBLE
a capstone imprint

First Facts is published by Pebble,
1710 Roe Crest Drive, North Mankato, Minnesota 56003
www.capstonepub.com

Library of Congress Cataloging-in-Publication Data
Names: Boone, Mary, 1963- author.
Title: Buildings inspired by nature / by Mary Boone.
Description: North Mankato, Minnesota : Pebble, [2020] | Series: Inspired by nature | Audience: Ages 6-9. | Audience: K to grade 3. | Includes bibliographical references and index.
Identifiers: LCCN 2019006440| ISBN 9781977108364 (library binding) | ISBN 9781977110060 (pbk.) | ISBN 9781977108555 (ebook pdf)
Subjects: LCSH: Architecture—Technological innovations—Juvenile literature. | Biomimicry—Juvenile literature.
Classification: LCC NA2555 .B645 2020 | DDC 720--dc23
LC record available at https://lccn.loc.gov/2019006440

Editorial Credits
Abby Colich and Jaclyn Jaycox, editors; Juliette Peters, designer; Jo Miller, media researcher; Katy LaVigne, production specialist

Photo Credits
b=bottom, i=inset, l=left, m=middle, r=right, t=top
Alamy: Thomas Cockram, 9r; Newscom: Reuters/Regis Duvignau, 19b; Science Source: Biophoto Associates, 11i, Lynwood M. Chace, 17l, Sebastian Kaulitzki, 15b; Shutterstock: arousa, 11, Celso Diniz, 13r, gnohz, 1m, 15t, Jacob Lund, 5, Kati McKeon, 1r, 21b, Kiev.Victor, 7l, Marko25, 19t, NERTHUZ, 7r, Pamela Brick, 17r, Rowan Denn, 9l, WDG Photo, Cover, William Perugini, 21t; Wikimedia: NOAA Photo Library, 11, 13l

Design Elements
Shutterstock: Zubada

Printed and bound in China.
001671

Table of Contents

From Nature to Buildings

Designers are always looking for new ideas. They want to make buildings stronger and safer. They look for ways to make them easier to heat and cool. Nature is one place they find new ideas. This is called biomimicry.

Fact

The word "biomimicry" comes from Greece. "Bios" means life. "Mimesis" means to copy.

Leg Bone to Eiffel Tower

The Eiffel Tower is one of the most famous places in the world. The human leg **inspired** its design. The tower is tall and thin like a leg bone. Braces support the tower. Muscles and **tissues** support the leg the same way.

inspire—to influence and encourage someone to do something

tissue—a layer or bunch of soft material that makes up body parts

Fact
About 7 million people visit the Eiffel Tower each year.

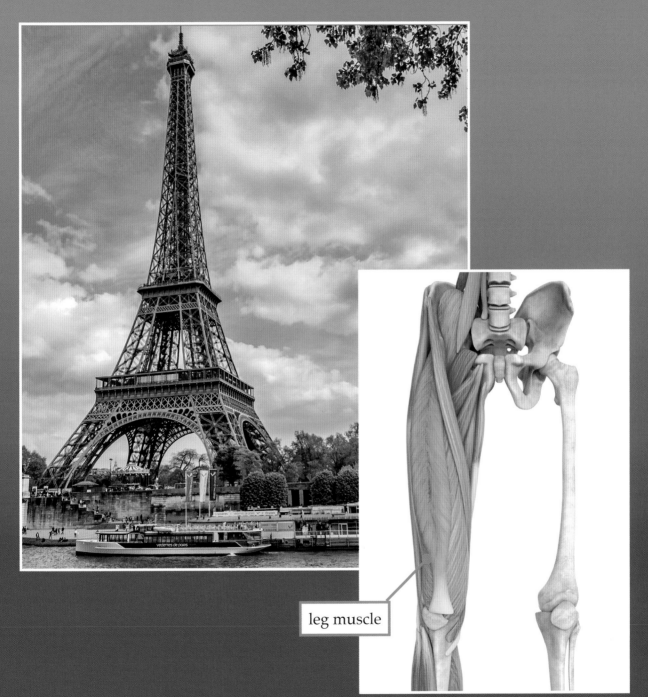

leg muscle

Termite Mound to Shopping Center

Some termites build huge **mounds**. The mounds are filled with **vents**. The insects open and close the vents. This controls the temperature. An **architect** used this idea. He designed a shopping center in Zimbabwe. Vents help cool the building. It doesn't need air conditioning.

architect—a person who designs buildings

mound—a hill or pile; some termites makes nests in tall mounds on the ground

vent—a long, narrow passage

Fact

Some termite mounds are very tall. They can reach more than 30 feet (9.1 meters).

Eastgate Centre
in Zimbabwe

9

Mussels to Waterproof Glue

Mussels make a sticky goo. The goo helps them hold onto rocks underwater. Scientists studied this goo. They made a new strong, safe glue. It can hold things together when it's wet. The glue may soon be used to make buildings stronger and safer.

sticky goo

Sea Life to Skyscrapers

Venus's Flower Basket is a sea sponge. This animal lives deep in the ocean. To eat it pulls water through holes. The Gherkin skyscraper is based on this animal. Air flows through the building like water flows through the sea sponge. This design makes the building easier to heat and cool.

carbon dioxide—a gas in the air that animals give off and plants use to make food

exoskeleton—a hard outer shell on some animals that protects them

Tough as Coral

Other sea animals inspire scientists too. A coral takes in **carbon dioxide**. The animal uses the gas. It makes a hard **exoskeleton**. A new kind of cement works the same way. It could help take extra carbon dioxide out of the air.

Petals to Paint

Lotus flower petals look smooth. But up close they are bumpy. The bumps keep dirt off the petals. Scientists have made a new house paint. It has bumps like lotus petals. Dirt won't stick to the paint. Buildings stay cleaner.

lotus flower surface

Taproots to Towers

Some plants have **taproots**. A large, center root helps hold up the plant. Smaller roots stick out. The SC Johnson Wax research tower was built like a taproot. Elevators and **ducts** form the center. They support the rest of the building.

Fact
Frank Lloyd Wright designed the tower. He was known for his designs inspired by nature.

duct—a tube, pipe, or channel that carries a liquid or air

taproot—the main root of certain plants, such as a carrot

Sunflowers to Solar Panels

Solar panels change sunlight into **electricity**. Homes and businesses use the electricity. Sunflowers move to follow the sun. They inspired new solar panels. The panels move. They always face the sun. They take in more sunlight. They create more electricity.

Algae House

One wall of Germany's "Algae House" is covered with algae. The algae clean out **pollutants**. They let out oxygen into the air.

---

electricity—a natural force that can be used to make light and heat or to make machines work

pollutant—a harmful material that can damage the environment

Forest to a Church

Architect Antoni Gaudí lived in Spain in the late 1800s. Sagrada Familia church is one of his most famous buildings. Forests inspired its inside. Columns look like trees with branches. The branches help support the ceiling.

Fact

Nature inspired another church in Italy. An architect studied an egg's shell. He designed the dome on a church in Florence, Italy. It is rounded and strong like an eggshell.

Glossary

architect (AR-ki-tekt)—a person who designs buildings

carbon dioxide (KAHR-buhn dy-AHK-syd)—a gas in the air that animals give off and plants use to make food

duct (DUHKT)—a tube, pipe, or channel that carries a liquid or air

electricity (i-lek-TRIS-i-tee)—a natural force that can be used to make light and heat or to make machines work

exoskeleton (ek-soh-SKE-luh-tuhn)—a hard outer shell on some animals that protects them

inspire (in-SPIRE)—to influence and encourage someone to do something

mound (MOUND)—a hill or pile; termites makes nests in tall mounds on the ground

pollutant (puh-LOOT-uhnt)—a harmful material that can damage the environment

taproot (TAP-root)—the main root of certain plants, such as a carrot

tissue (TISH-yoo)—a layer or bunch of soft material that makes up body parts

vent (VENT)—a long, narrow passage

Read More

Bell, Samantha S. *Everyday Inventions Inspired by Nature*. Technology Inspired by Nature. Mendota Heights, MN: Focus Readers, 2018.

Jones, Grace. *The Greatest Buildings and Structures*. Ideas, Inventions, and Innovators. New York: Crabtree, 2019.

Koontz, Robin. *Biomimic Building*. Nature-Inspired Innovations. Vero Beach, FL: Rourke Educational Media, 2018.

Internet Sites

Everyday Mysteries: Biomimicry for Kids
https://www.loc.gov/rr/scitech/mysteries/biomimicry.html

How We Make Stuff
https://www.made2bmadeagain.org/creatures_cwdtd

You! Be Inspired!: Nature Inspired Architectural Designs
http://www.ucreative.com/inspiration/you-be-inspired-10-nature-inspired-architectural-designs/

Critical Thinking Questions

1. Which building is based on a sea sponge?

2. Why is it helpful to have solar panels that turn toward the sun?

3. Which building inspired by nature would you most like to visit? Why?

Index